I0759361

Judge Anna von Rietz Interview
Taking Back America

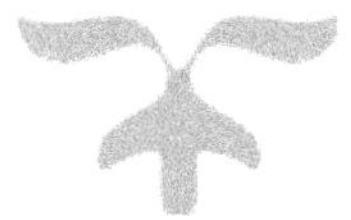

Copyrighted on the 4th of March 2018

By: Anna Maria Riezinger

TRANSCRIPT OF
VIDEO REMOVED FROM THE INTERNET
www.tinyurl.com/yc6a6gdo

THIS FULL Judge Anna Von Reitz Interview Was Requested By Many To Be Uploaded As ONE Video File.

Victurus Libertas VL
Published on Dec 6, 2017

We received a lot of requests from our subscribers as well as Judge Anna herself to offer this as one large file so here it is in Transcript Form. We are very fortunate and grateful that Judge Anna granted us this interview. We hope this has enlightened some of you to the truth - Jim & Angie Blake.

Here's Judge Anna's website:
www.annavonreitz.com

Here's Judge Anna's snail mail:
**Anna Maria Riezinger
c/o Box 520994
Big Lake, Alaska 99652**

Here's Judge Anna's PayPal:
avannavon@gmail.com

Judge Anna von Rietz Interview
Taking Back America

Victurus Libertas VL
"If God is for us, who can be against us?"

ANGIE: Hey guys, I'm so excited tonight! Our guest is a State Superior Court Judge. She's an author and advocate of our original Republic, and an educator to so many thru her website: *annavonreitz.com*. We're delighted to have her on our show tonight: *Judge Anna von Reitz.*

JIM: Hey, Judge Anna! How are you?

Angie: Thank you! Okay. So Judge Anna, Um. We have been Fans of your's for so long and thank you so much for being here. And we would like to start with you and I, like you said, we've been researching this kind of stuff for a long time. But we have a lot of Newbies to get familiar with our Channel. So what we'd like to do is explain to them: where we came from, where we are right now, and where we might be going as a civilization. Can you help us with that?

ANNA: Well I can try. Basically things got off-track during the Civil War.

Now, we have always been taught to call it the "Civil War" but it wasn't actually a war, it was a Military Conflict, and there is a difference.

I guess the way to put it is that in a lawful war there is a Declaration, and there is an End. There is a Peace Treaty.

But in a Commercial Conflict where you've got Mercenaries on both sides, it's not that clean-cut kind of affair. It's an illegal war. Let's put it that way. And it does not have the standing nor the repercussions nor the meaning of a true war. So what happened here in the 1860s was not a war, even though that's what we call it, it was not. It was a Commercial Mercenary Conflict. And the reason that we can be sure that this is true is that there was no formal Declaration of any War by the Congress, ever, and there was no official Peace Treaty ending it, either. Those two things which should be there, aren't there. And I can pretty much definitively challenge anybody with a million dollar reward to find any actual Declaration by Congress making any war, or an actual Peace Treaty ending it.

ANGIE: And I don't want to interrupt, but do we have those in all these other wars?

Anna: Yes!

Angie: We do! Okay. Alright. Good.

Anna: But it's questionable that those other wars were lawful either, because the entities that were involved that were actually making these declarations don't appear to be lawful government entities. They all appear to be corporations and operating as corporations.

And when a corporation... when a government steps out and assumes the character of a commercial corporation, it loses all claims of governing and becomes just another commercial corporation. So it would be like IBM declaring War on GM, that sort of a "war" as kind of euphemistic thing like the so-called "War on Drugs", and wars on all these other things, like the "War on Terrorism". And this just keeps the pretense of war going forward.

They're pretending that they're at war, but they're corporations, and can't declare a real war. So what they're doing is basically a bunch of legalistic chicaneries and semantic deceits in order to bring forward false claims.

Essentially the same thing happened to us with our Estates.

After the war, the southern States were in ruins, and the northern States were bankrupt, thanks to Lincoln. And the Grand Army of the Republic, which is what they called the Union Army, was in charge under a set of rules that were set up in 1863 called the Lieber Code. Now, the Lieber Code has since morphed into the Hague Conventions.

And that's another whole story I won't go into.

Essentially we have a situation where we have the actual states and natural people and the actual government that we are owed which we all think of as the United States. Right?

Then we have the Municipal United States which was a government allowed to Congress under the original constitution to rule over the Washington, D.C. Municipality. OK?

So they were given the right to have their very own oligarchy and take control of Washington, D.C. which they then parlayed into an international City-State.

They have their own little baileywick over there which is called the Municipal United States.

And then finally we have the Territorial United States which is still run by the military.

(WOW!)

So we go off and we're virtually unaware of all this. Right?

(RIGHT)

So we've got three different governments, the United States of America (unincorporated), the United States Municipality, and the Territorial United States.

And all these things are happening all around us all the time and they're all feeding off of us because they all get their money from us. Right?

(RIGHT.)

So we've been carrying around all of these different levels of government, plus county government, plus municipal and government-funded boroughs and counties, you know, you name it, and last but not least, they're trying to foist off

Regional government on us, too, through the United Nations.

So each one of these levels of government goes out and they play a game. It's really kind of funny because what they do is, they describe you or they describe your property, and they infringe on your common law copyright in order to do it, by describing... I'll give you an example with property.

Say that your house is identified as 911 Spring Street. OK?

And it has another property description that the tax assessor gives it which might be # 9-2014, Plat # 8-B, of the Springfield County Plat. OK?

Or it might a municipal designation, like, Lot 12, Block 3, of the Fairyland Park Subdivision, you know. They keep changing all these different descriptions.

That's what they are Foreclosing on. They're not foreclosing on your house.

(THEY'RE DESCRIPTIONS? THEY'RE DESCRIPTIONS THAT THEY HAVE? WOW!)

Yes. They just copyright the description, and then they arbitrarily claim that that description is theirs, and they have the copyrights and the descriptions to prove it. Right?

They put that in as a "title"-- a "title" like a title to a book. And then they foreclose on that "title".

(HUH? INTERESTING.)

It's all just chicanery. It's all fraud.

(THAT'S THE SAME THING THEY'VE DONE WITH PEOPLE TOO, RIGHT? CAN YOU GO THROUGH THAT A LITTLE BIT WITH THE BIRTH CERTIFICATE?)

Right. Well, they do the same thing with the Birth Certificate. What's supposed to happen is that when a baby is born, the parents are supposed to give Notice to the community, and copyright the baby's name. Basically nail down the common law copyright of the child's name by recording it.

To "Record" anything puts it in the Land Jurisdiction. To "Register" anything puts it in the Sea Jurisdiction.

(HUH.)

But because our parents don't know this, and they aren't told this, they don't do it. They might write your name down in the family Bible, and that does create a record, but that's not a public record of you holding your own name and everything.

So instead, what happens is that the hospital posts your given name in a birth announcement.

If after however long, a week, two weeks, whatever, nobody comes forward to claim that baby, the hospital then turns it over as an Abandoned Vessel by that very name.

And it gets registered by that "State of" organization. Basically the Department of Health and Human Services (DHHS). And you're considered a "Ward of the State" as though you had been left on the hospital's doorstep.

So they've copyrighted your given name. And on your birth certificate you will see that the actual name is in all capital letters, and that's how you make a corporation, a corporate entity. It could be a Corporation, it could be a State, it could be a Trust of any kind, a Nation, a C-corp, an LLC, all of those things are named with all capital letters.

So when we see that birth certificate, you'll notice that's your actual birth day mentioned, and then, there's a filing date, which is always a few days or weeks later.

Well, the Birth **Day** is the record of you being born.

And the Birth **Date** is the record of the Thing, the Estate, or public transmitting utility, or cooperative, or whatever else is registered. That's Its Birth Date.

[People have birthdays; persons, that is, corporate entities, have birthdates.]

The birth certificate has two functions.

Its first function is as an Insurance Indemnity Receipt.

When they seize your property they have to insure you against loss and damage. So when they purloin your property like this, it's called a usufruct where they make use of your property and assets for their benefit. So they have to insure you against loss or damage. OK?

So your birth certificate is an Indemnity Insurance Receipt. OK?

And the other thing it is, it's a Bond.

A lot of people are confused about what bonds are. A bond is an I.O.U. It has no value but what you give it.

And they figured out using accounting and actuarial tables how much money you might be expected to earn on average or make in a lifetime, and they bond your Estate for that amount. That includes your labor, whatever you might accrue as homeowner or tax, blah, blah, blah.

So they put this I.O.U. out there, this bond in your name -- the all capital letter name -- the Estate name -- and then they sit back and benefit from trading that name, and from putting insurance policies on it and collecting on that.

One of the most repulsive things that they do is they take your money that you spend on taxes and things of that nature and they take out a life insurance policy on you so that when you die, they get paid!

(WOW! JUDGE ANNA DO YOU HAVE A BIRTH CERTIFICATE? OR HAVE YOU REMEDIED THIS IN SOME WAY FOR YOURSELF?)

Well, since it's an Insurance Indemnity Receipt, it's actually a very good tool for you, once you figure out this game.

So now you know what a birth certificate is.

Now you go and get that birth certificate authenticated. And that is a process of going to the state Secretary of State with a birth certificate and saying, OK, I want your office to authenticate that this is a genuine actual birth certificate.

So the state Secretary of State goes through and says everything checks out, and Boom! they stamp it, and they put a cover sheet on the birth certificate you got from Vital Statistics. And then next, you take it to the United States Secretary of State, in this case, Rex Tillerson's new office, and you do the same thing, you say, "Hey, I want this authenticated." And they go through the same process, and they put their cover sheet on top of it.

So what you get back at the end of the day is the three-page document. It has the US Secretary of State's verification that it is a genuine article. You have the State Secretary of State's verification that it is a genuine article. And you have the birth certificate that you got from the Vital Statistics people. And so you've now... as I call it... you've built the Lawnmover.

You now have the absolute proof that this is what was done. This is who did it to you. And this is who is liable for having done that to you. Alright?

That's step One. So you now have an authenticated birth certificate.

Now, just briefly, a lot of people have questions. Why is it Authenticated? Why is it Certified. Why was it not Apostilled?

Well the plain fact of the matter is that there are different Conventions that different groups of countries have for guaranteeing the authenticity of documents that pass back and forth between them in international business. And all of the Hague Convention countries actually do this for themselves for the purpose of guaranteeing that their records are correct.

But all the countries that never signed on to the Hague Convention, including the United States of America, need authentication.

So that's why when you are acting as an American State National, you're acting under the auspices of the United States of America, not the United States.

And this is why you have to authenticate your birth certificate for use in international trade instead of getting an apostille.

And people get run around by a State Secretary of State's office to have to do an authentication. Some of them balk at it and say, What's that?

But that's just their ignorance coming out. And we have to keep on them and make sure they continue to do their job.

So anyway, that's why it's an authentication instead of an apostille. And when you want an authentication you tell these State Secretary of State and U.S. Secretary of State office people that you need it for doing business in Indonesia or one of the other countries that never signed on to the Hague Convention. And that's really all that is necessary.

So anyway, that's why you get it authenticated and that's the overall purpose, just to have a copy of a document that's guaranteed to be genuine. So you can go into any court and they can't walk over and say, "Oh well, this isn't quite official", you know, and give you all that other runaround.

You have to go back and claim your trade-name and your estate that is copyrighted by the British Crown Corporation.

They hold it only in secondary capacity because you were born before their franchise. It's first in line, first in time, in commerce.

You are the Holder in due Course. You have first dibs, on your Christian trade-name, which is your first, middle, and last, upper and lower case name that you were always taught to use in grade school.

So you go back in and claim back your own name, using a common law copyright going back all the way to your birthday. And you re-convey your property to the land and soil of the State where you were born.

We have a form called a Certificate of Assumed Name that does all this, plus it gives you a standing Writ of Habeas Corpus established on the public record. And once that's done and it's recorded, you have control of not only your trade-name but all of the derivative names that were spun off of it.

You now have control of the "Strawman" that is named in all capital letters, first, middle, and last, and the public transmitting utility name which is upper and lower case, or it can be all caps with nothing but a middle initial. [And the original Public Trust—the Ward of the State name, which is just your first and last, upper and lower case.]

And there are all sorts of different variations. Last name first, First name last, Upper and middle lower case, all caps with a middle initial, without a middle initial, with this punctuation, with that punctuation, it doesn't matter.

These are all different derivatives of your Christian Trade-Name. So you claim them all. You claim the whole thing. Your Trade-Name and every variation possible. OK?

And at the same time, you establish a Writ of Habeas Corpus that allows you to go into their court and take over administratively and basically tell them what to do, instead of them administering your estate, laying down the law and fining you and putting you in jail.

You tell them what you're going to do!

You walk in and you say, Hey! I'm the subrogee of the defendant. I'm the priority creditor, I'm the paramount security interest holder, and guess what? you're not!

So now that we have it straightened out about who I am and what my role is, I am owed all the bonds that the prosecutor brought forward and I want all charges eliminated!

There is not a thing they can do about it. Boom! That's it!

[If you have your paperwork done and do it properly.]

(WHAT HAPPENS IF OUT OF IGNORANCE THEY DON'T CARE AND THEY JUST THROW YOU IN JAIL ANYWAY, OUT OF FORCE?)

Well, we have had examples of that happening and there are some very ignorant judges out there. Most judges realize that what they're doing in those courts has nothing to do with the actual law. It's just an administrative process. But there are some who are corrupt and there are some who are ignorant.

And we do wind up with some cases of them in one way or another presuming and imposing on people under false presumption and false pretenses.

However we now have enforcement... needing to do this one county at a time.

Oh yes, we still need to do this one county at a time in order to restore our true government to its full functioning under the land law. We need to get our butts up off the couch and form our County Jural Assemblies. Right?

The First Amendment doesn't say, peaceably "associate" so we're talking about a Jural "Assembly", not a Jural "Society". OK? [Jural Societies support Maritime and Admiralty Courts, Jural Assemblies support land jurisdiction courts.]

Because the assembly is what forms the courts on the land jurisdiction, and we the living people are land jurisdiction beings, we function and control the land jurisdictions of our country.

Why are we land assets and land beings? Number One, we're born on the land. Number Two, "from dust thou art, and unto dust thou returnest".

So we come from the land and as a result, we are land beings and land assets, and guess what? We are owed the Law of the Land. Alright?

You have to step back a little bit and think about this in terms of land and sea. Land is the International Jurisdiction.

And what are nations in this country? Our States are our Nations. Every State is a Nation. So you are born as a Minnesotan, or a Wisconsinite, or a Mainer, or a Texan, or a Californian. Whatever. This is your Nationality.

More generally, of course, we call ourselves Americans. But "American" is kind of a melting pot term that could apply to anyone in the continental North or South America. Right?

It could be somebody in, you know---Venezuela.

American isn't terribly useful because of that. It's much more to the point when you're talking about nationality, to look 'em right in the eye and say, I'm a Minnesotan. That's my Nation. And this is my nation-state. OK?

The actual land that you're standing on is your nation-state. And you have control of your national land jurisdiction. OK?

So this is something that Americans have to remember too.

Over the years it's become... they... consider yourself kind of all together. Right? --That there is no separation or differences and it's all just one big thing, but that only happens in international jurisdiction.

What happens is that these original states saw the benefit of combining their responsibility and delegating those responsibilities. So what they did was they formed essentially what we would recognize today as a Holding Company. An unincorporated Holding Company called The United States of America. This Holding Company holds all of the state's international jurisdictions both on the land and on the sea.

And out of this slush pile of international powers, they delegated 19 of those powers to the [Territorial] United States, and so the [Territorial] United States was [and is] a separate government controlled by Britain.

They came in here as purveyors of governmental services.

So their entire role was to come here and provide us with good-faith services to provide us with these 19 governmental services which are called powers.

But the exercise of those powers results in a commercial service contract, and that is essentially what the Constitution did. It set up that whole deal. It set up the United States Government. It set up the commercial services contract which delegates the 19 powers so that entity [the United States Government] could provide those 19 services. [Instead of each state providing their own and each coming up with something different.]

And the United States of America retained all the different powers that were not specifically enumerated. So the U.S.A. stands above the U.S. and always has. The United States of America, which is an unincorporated body politic and an unincorporated Holding Company has always had the primary role and responsibility over the U.S.

And that's the way it's designed, and that's why you have Amendment Ten which says that all rights that are not specifically delegated are retained by the states and the people.

And the United States of America that delegated those powers is in the position to take those powers back if the United States fails to live up to its contract, if it welches, if it breaches, if it fails to perform, we have the ability and the responsibility to say, "Joe Blow? You have a contract with us and you didn't do what you said you were going to do, you went bankrupt, we don't accept the successor to your bankruptcy, and you put yourself in the position of... liken it to a Condominium Association. You're familiar with how Condos work. Right?

You have something which looks like large apartment complex, but every "apartment" in [that complex] is actually its own little world, it's own little house, within this larger framework. Well, it's the same way with the States and the USA. OK?

So you go out and you hire somebody to take care of the condominium grounds, the jointly shared grounds.

You've got this company that comes in, and they trim the trees, and they take out the garbage, and they do the snow plowing, and all that other stuff. They provide these services. These 19 enumerated services. They're out there and they're doing their job, and Boom! that company goes bankrupt. Alright?

So what happens?

Well I can tell you what did happen. This company went bankrupt, then another company showed up, was booted up by the same exact people. Another company was booted up.

They changed the name slightly, and they changed the color of the truck, and they came right back in there and continued doing all of these jobs. Right?

And if you don't object, then a process of Assumpsit takes place. They just assume the contract and they continue on doing their work, but it's a different company. And that's what's been happening here.

(IS THE FEDERAL RESERVE ONE OF THE ENTITIES THAT YOU'VE BEEN TALKING ABOUT?)

Sure. Absolutely.

(SO WHO'S IN CHARGE OF THE UNITED STATES OF AMERICA, WHO CAN SAY, WE'RE FIRING YOU, WE WANT TO GO BACK TO OUR SOVEREIGN WAYS?)

Well essentially, that's what has already happened, back in 2008.

First we have a company called the United States.

It goes bankrupt in 1863. They reorganize and they spawn another company called The United States of America, Inc., but that's not the United States of America which is an unincorporated body politic. [nor their unincorporated Holding Company]. It's an incorporated business named after us, infringing on our copyright and seeking to deceive people into thinking it is us. It should have been in all capital letters, but it wasn't. It was in upper and lower case and was identified as an Inc.,— as an incorporation.

Then that went bankrupt in 1907 as a corporation, and guess what? They flipped right around and they introduced the United States of America, Inc. with a small "t" on the "the".

They changed the name just a tiny bit. This is the kind of chicanery that we've been dealing with.

So the company that was formed right after the Civil War was bankrupted in 1907. The perpetrator, the last one in line, was the United States of America with a small "t" on the "the", and that went from 1907 to 1933.

There was a period of time when the small "t" was operating and then it went bankrupt. And then we got the UNITED STATES (all caps).

That too was another incorporation, but this was a Municipal corporation of the Washington, D.C. Municipal corporation and the District of Columbia.

So you've got all these different providers of these services and they are charging us for all these services. And they're just running wild. There's nobody minding the store. The service providers are just selling us whatever services they want to provide for us and charging us and our states for all these services they a wracking up.

They've gotten to the point where they're charging us for the service of even incarcerating us. What these rascals, these cretins, were trying to do, they were setting up a situation similar to Nazi Germany where they were going to come in here and claim all of our property and assets and kill us off by the millions and collect the life insurance policies on us, and collect all of the "abandoned property" of the dead people who leave behind all this property, set up a concentration camp system, and just run us right thru it, and then charge the survivors for all these services that they do. And the people would not know this until it was right on them.

But thankfully, there were some of us who were awake, and had seen what went on in Nazi Germany and recognized the signs of it, and when they got down to buying millions of body bags and building 800 FEMA Camps and started running railroads to them, and buying millions of rounds of ammunition and distributing it to privately owned sub-contractors, like DARPA and the FBI, and FEMA and all these other alphabet soup agencies... which are not government... they're just sub-contractors of government. Then we raised our hands and we said, NO! enough of this. This is not going to happen. We're going to expose you from here to breakfast and go after you!

(So this happened around 2008???)

All this started with the end of the bankruptcy of the United States of America, Inc (the small "t" version) that F.D.R. booted up and bankrupted back in 1933.

That came out of bankruptcy back in 1999 and at that point, we raised our hand and said, EP! Hey guys! We're now home. We're back on the Land. And we're not messing around with you any more. And during the next 20 years various actions were taken to object.

It was during this time that we went all the way to Rome and banged our dish on the floor like angry dogs, and wound up talking to the Pope and doing all sorts of other things. And getting all sorts of paperwork done at the Hague. And various groups around the country got organized to restore their county and their state.

And all this has been going on . . . I mean this has been

happening now for 20-30 years and it has just now gotten to the critical Mass where enough people are informed so that they're concerned and they're actually taking a much more serious view and taking personal action. And during that time, the abuses of the courts and of the police, and the sub-contracting agencies have gotten worse, and the propaganda on the TV and radio has gotten worse.

And the cognitive dissonance between all the Yankee-doodle-dandy Land of the Free stuff and the actual gut wrenching fear that many people have felt when approached by the IRS or the FBI or some of these other agencies like the BATF grew. It all sounds very hollow now, doesn't it? You realize that you're being coerced and victimized and your rights are not being respected and that these people on your soil are causing trouble for you and you are employing them.

So who gets to boss me around? I would like to know just exactly what is the basis of this premise that you think that you can come in here and tell me what to do when I'm paying your salary. Hello? America?

(OUR COURT SYSTEM IS UNDER MARITIME LAW?)

OK! If you think about it in terms of land and sea, Maritime is the interstice between the actual sea and the land.

There's that intertidal zone, that's Maritime, that's commerce. That's the Merchant Marine Service. You've heard of the Merchant Marines?

These guys have their own law, their own thing going on. And then you have Admiralty. That's the High Seas, That's out away from that intertidal zone where you're actually outside of any country's sphere of influence and you're in true International Jurisdiction, and that's all under the Queen.

(DO WE HAVE THAT HERE IN THE UNITED STATES?)

Absolutely! It's part of our court system now. No! I should say, it's part of THEIR court system. We get sucked into their court system via their franchises. Have you ever studied their Magic at all? or any of that at all? Because there's a thing in the tradition of Magic called the Poppet, like a voo-doo doll?

Well, the Strawman functions like a Poppet or voo-doo doll. They use it like a handle to grab hold of your assets and control you and your assets without actually addressing you. And that's how they get away with it. Because there's no law against raping, pillaging, murdering, and stealing from, a corporation, [which is] a fiction, and they're all dealing in fiction. So you can't tell them they harmed any fiction because a fiction doesn't exist.

(SO HOW DO YOU BRING THEM BACK TO REALITY?)

You claim the copyright to your trade-name and all of its derivatives and all of its punctuations and its variations and then you sit back and go, "Hey! I am the Subrogee, I am the the Priority Creditor." So basically, you're claiming yourself back. You're claiming your Name and your Estate. Your Estate is attached to your Name.

Right now, according to the government, we're just individual corporations. You died a long long time ago. All what's left of you is your Estate. You haven't been heard from since you left that hospital.

This is how they get away with extorting income tax from us, because we're corporations [so far as the falsified public records show].

100% of the Income Tax applies only to corporations. In fact, the word "income" is specifically and only applicable to corporations. Such an income tax is against a corporation. By definition it cannot be a tax against a living being.

In 77,000 pages of the IRS tax code, not one time do they define what income is, because they can't [define it honestly].

But it has been defined by the Supreme Court as "profit severed from capital".

The real shtick separated here is that income applies to corporate accrual. By definition it applies only to corporate accruals.

Well they'll try anything! These people are just private bill collectors. They have no governmental authority.

Let me give you a little run-down on the History of the income tax. It began in the 1100s in England and France. It was called Peter's Pence. It was an income tax that was created by the Roman Catholic Church to pay for the Crusades and it was collected by their special bill collectors who were black-robed men who wore white wigs. They were called "Galli" and they were priests of the pagan goddess Cybele that came to Rome in the 2nd Century BC and they've been bill collectors for the Pope and Roman Pontiff ever since.

So on the 15th of every April they'd come around and they would collect an income tax called Peter's Pence. And they're still doing the same thing now. Only they're doing it through the Internal Revenue Service and they're using Judges and Barristers. And you will note that the British Barristers still wear white wigs just like the Galli, so it's all connected all across history and if you'll start studying history you'll see that nothing much has changed.

The income tax has always been illegal in America, but it is not illegal in the [Territorial] United States. So they can't charge us living people anything, but they can charge their incorporated "PERSON" [named after you without your knowledge or consent] however much they want as long as you let them have a corporate "person" to control.

Specific names: *person, man, woman, human.* The word "human" (*hue of man*) means the color of man in the sense of the color of law. It appears to be a man, but it is not. So you don't want people calling you a human (noun) because one of the definitions of a human is a monster like a strawman. Something that appears to be a man but isn't. Such as Sasquatch!

You're not even sure it exists, but if it does, does it have rights? And why should it have rights? Maybe it's an animal and only appears to be a man. I'm for animal rights and I don't think anything should be cruelly treated, but I'm not going to go out there and stand and stake my rights on a claim that is questionable.

I want my natural and unquestionable God-given rights, thank you.

I started studying this back in the '70s when I caught a broadcast during the confirmation hearings of Nelson Rockefeller as Gerry Ford's V.P. I was home one day and just happened to turn on the TV and a Committee was all seated in the Rotunda and they were talking to Nelson Rockefeller asking him questions, and the question came up, Hey, Mr. R, how much money did you make last year in personal income?

And he said something like, Oh "$480 million." I don't recall exactly but it was a lot back then. And the next question was, how much in federal income tax did you pay?

And he stood there just as stony faced as you please and he said, "None!"

And you could almost hear the breath go out of everyone in the room. Right?

And then the Chairman of the Committee who was doing the questioning fussed around in his chair a little bit and leaned over and he said: "Are we to understand that you had $480 million dollars, and blah, blah, blah, and you didn't pay any federal income tax at all?"

And Nelson just kind of sat back in his chair and said, "None."

(THEY HAVE KNOWN ABOUT THIS GAME FOR A LONG TIME.)

So this little girl in Wisconsin thought let's see, I just paid 1/3rd of my little wages in my pay check to the federal government for all these different federal taxes, and he made all that money and he paid Zero? Now I want to know what he knows.

So this takes wading through the federal code and it is literally Code.

So this federalese language is probably the very worst gobbledy-gook on the planet that you're ever going to read. And throughout the IRS Code I kept coming up with such terms as "non-resident alien". And for most American it would never ever occur to them that they were by any means a non-resident alien. I mean that's like you talking about someone who comes over from Mexico and does a day trip and goes back home as a non-resident alien.

Huh! So that's what the federal Code uses to refer to us. And you have to flip it around on its head and look at it from their perspective as a foreign government.

They're a foreign government and you're reading their Code now. You are a "non-resident alien." So first you have to catch on to things like that as you're reading their gobbledy-gook which is deliberatiely and horribly deceptive, convoluted, and utterly messed up.

(INTENTIONALLY!)

I plowed through over 125,000 pages of that Code and by the time I got done with that, I had an education in federalese.

I still was clinging to my naive belief in America, "Land of the Free", and I realized that I was being bamboozled somehow and I had a pretty good idea that it wasn't good, and that I had caught on to some of it.

And at that time I was running an art gallery. My husband is an artist. A fine artist. A member of the Oil Painters of America and has been for a long long time. We have our own art gallery.

So I was a good little person, I made up all these questions about a change that we were looking at, an expansion for our business, and I had questions about how that would affect taxation.

So I took all these questions into the local IRS office and made an appointment with the top dog at the IRS office and I went into the office and asked all these questions and wrote the answers down. And I said, "I think I understand this, would you go back over and read the questions and the answers you gave me and initial it. Do I have it right?"

"Oh No! I couldn't do that," he said.

(THERE CAN'T BE ANY ACCOUNTABLILITY.)

That would be like going to, say, the Department of Natural Resources and asking, "When was Moose season this year?" And they say, "Well, September 30th to October 10th." And you ask them to write that out and confirm that to give you something to prove that, and they won't. So I knew right then and there, that things were messed up. That's how I knew that it was a Scam. And that was the most horrifying scary moment that you can think of. It was as if I had been at the top of a really tall roller coaster, and having the bottom fall out.

(SO THIS IS A SCAM IN THE TAX SYSTEM, AND THEN YOU STARTED LEARNING MORE, RIGHT, AND IT DIDN'T GET BETTER, DID IT?)

It just got worse and worse. And the path went up and down and all around into different areas and I found out that as a result of the 1907 bankruptcy all of our land had been held as sureties for that bankruptcy.

They came and they laid claim to all of our land and they parcelled it out either as residential, industrial, or agricultural, and they took title to all that land - all of it - as surety for the bankruptcy that started in 1907.

When that bankruptcy settled in 1953 the rats said, "Oh, we can't possibly know who this land actually belongs to any more." So they put it into two giant Trusts.

The Department of Agriculture . . . and the public land was ground up by the Department of the Interior . . . and it was managed by the Bureau of Land Management.

So they took title to all of our land as surety for their debt, and then made a false claim of abandonment and wrote it all over into trusts, and they continued to hold the title.

So they stole our land by this chicanery which was nothing but open fraud, and then pulled the same thing with our labor, our labor assets, and our personal and private property, with the 1933 bankruptcy.

That was when they stole our actual silver dollars, the value of our labor, our name, all of it. They used all that as sureties for their debt, too. And they . . . Ah . . . They're nothing but a bunch of rotten criminal no-goods.

(IT'S THE CROWN, THE ROCKEFELLERS, & THE ROTHSCHILDS WHO ACTUALLY STARTED ALL THESE SCAMS?)

There are actuallly two colluding Gangs involved. There's a Dutch Gang and there's an English Gang, that started all this. And then overtime the Dutch Gang included some French elements.

So we've got Western European Countries and corporate governments fooling around with this, and trying to seize upon our assets by this legal chicanery.

(SO THESE BANKRUPTCIES THAT YOU'RE TALKING ABOUT, ARE THESE MISMANAGEMENT, OR ARE THESE PLANNED BANKRUPTCIES?)

These are planned bankruptcies. They happen in a cyclical fashion every 70 to 80 years, and they are set up so that they can discharge their debt against us, leaving us holding the bag for their debt. So we become indebted to their debt and they continue to hold us as Wards of their State . . . of the last generation's service provider.

(IS IT POSSIBLE THAT THIS MIGHT HAPPEN AGAIN? NOW WHAT ARE WE, $20 TRILLION DOLLARS IN DEBT? AND IS THIS MONEY BEING HELD OFF-SHORE?)

OK. That $20 trillion dollars is their debt. It's not our debt.

It's their debt. So the next question is: If there's a $20 trillion dollar national debt, whose holding the credit? Because in a debt/credit system, every time you pay a debt with a debt you create a credit. Right?

You actually never get paid in this system until you foist off their debt notes on someone else. So credit is created for one party, and debt is created for the receiving party. It's backwards from anything that you normally think of, because your trading a debt like a negative number. I'm holding a negative $7 and I give you that negative $7 as a payment of a $7 debt, so now you got negative $14 dollars in your pocket, and yet we're spending this as if it is real and as if this made any sense. Right?

It doesn't. It's just a bookkeeping fiasco thats all.

So you know that if there's a $20 trillion dollar debt, somebody is holding the other side of that as a $20 trillion dollar credit. But you never hear about the National Credit, do you?

Well the answer is that you hold the $20 trillion dollar credit, and they're not doing their bookkeeping by bringing the 2 sides of it together to zero it out. It's bookkeeping fraud, essentially. They've already received payment. There is no National Debt. Think of it. What happened? Is it possible to have a transaction that doesn't zero out? To alter a contract stipulating otherwise?

I go to the store. I buy $10 worth of gas. I give them the $10 dollars and they give me the gas. It zeros out. So this idea that there can be a $20 trillion dollar National Debt without there being a $20 trillion dollar National Credit is bogus. It always has been. And yet they've pumped this up no end trying to make an excuse for why the American people should pay it again, and its nothing but BS.

It's dishonest bookkeeping, and it began as a result of Fast Eddie Ohara. Fast Eddie Ohara was Al Capone's bookkeeper. And he set up a new bookkeeping system which is known as "Cooking the Books" or keeping 2 Sets of books. Double Accrual bookkeeping instead of Carriage bookkeeping. And quess who adopted Fast Eddie Ohara's bookkeeping system in 1946?

The US Government !

The General Accounting Office switched over to Double Accrual bookkeeping. And they haven't kept it straight since.

(THEY WERE INDICTING THOSE PEOPLE, AND THEY SAID, IT'S A GOOD IDEA WHAT THEY'RE DOING. WE'LL INDICT THEM. THEN WE'LL DO WHAT THEY'RE DOING)

The FBI found out about Al Capones bookkeepong system in the '20s, and by 1946 all the government corporations had adopted it.

(SO WHAT WE'RE TALKING ABOUT UP 'TILL NOW IS PRETTY BLACK, BUT THERE IS GOOD NEWS, RIGHT? YOU SEE GOOD NEWS IN THE FUTURE? THERE'S BEEN AN AWAKENING? RIGHT? DURING THE LAST 10 YEARS OR LESS?)

Well, let's see. An awful lot of people have started taking charge of the IRS. And they're no longer the Bully Boys they were, as a result.

So... Because . . . When you're well informed and well armed and you know Buckwheat . . . and you know how to write a letter . . . you can claim your Exemption and kick them right out of your life.

And you can even do it 10 years retroactivity. You have no obligation to the IRS unless you are a federal employee or a federal dependent. And, basically, what that means is that there are certain people who are legitimately federal citizens. People who are in the military, military dependents, federal civilian employees and their dependents, people who are legitimate wards of the state, like people who are in insane asylums, Um, you know. This is who this applies to.

And also, unfortunately, black Americans.

After the Civil War, the slaves were never actually granted state citizenship. The rotten no good governmental services corporation that booted up in the wake of the Civil War came in and claimed title to the black plantation slaves that had been supposedly freed!

The British Crown came right back in after the fact, claimed title to them, and what happened is that all although Private slave ownership was outlawed, Public slave ownership had just begun!

But it was actually from that, that all the rest of this has happened. Because we were not sharp enough to figure out what these rats were doing, and object to it and put a stop to it. They re-enslaved the black people, the plantation slaves, as public slaves. Then they extended this to all federal employees of the US. They have been able to work this out by controlling the courts and by controlling the banks.

(TALKING ABOUT BANKS, WHAT DO WE SEE AS FAR AS THE FUTURE OF THE MONETARY SYSTEM, CRIPTO CURRENCY, AND THE CASHLESS SOCIETY THAT WE SEE COMING IN?)

Well OK. I don't believe in money. I never have. To me it's a ridiculous concept. It's just absolutely stupid, you know. Give me this little piece of metal stamped with something on it, and tell me that that's worth three bushels of wheat. Ya, right. Who? How? What? This makes no sense.

And I used to go round and round with one of my friends about the paper in your wallet. Then take it out and have this bill in front of me and say, look, this is just paper! And you can't even make it toilet paper. You can't write a note on it. It's useless! It's worthless. What are you doing? What are you thinking?

You're slaving your life away for this?

It's stupid. Well, it is.

It's just more flim flam. It's more what...?

I call it idolatry!

Because what happens is that people don't have the sophistication and the discernment to make a distinction between a symbol of value and actual value. Whatever it is that's being used as a symbol of value becomes synonymous with the actual value in their minds.

And that's a logic mistake of major proportions that then offers the opportunity for flim-flam artists and conmen to come in and profit themselves.

And so, I think the entire concept of money is useless. And I think that this is just part of a greater problem, in that I keep encountering people who can't think, they can't feel, and because they can't feel they can't properly value anything. And this is a scary gigantic problem, worldwide.

Now you stop and observe. You know that you never feel anything except from what you think. Thought always precedes a feeling. You have to think something in order to feel anything.

Well, if your thinking is wrong, your feeling is wrong. And if your thought and feeling are wrong then you don't have the basis to judge the value of anything. I mean, how else can it be that we don't value a human life? How is that possible? Because our head is screwed up. It's because our feelings are not as they should be. I mean, we have to retrain ourselves to think, which will then allow us to feel, and when we get our thinking and feeling together, then we'll be able to look around and say, Oh. What Is really valuable?

Our value system is all screwed up. I am completly square with that. That's important, and our priorities are messed up as well. However, I was just...

(THERE'S SOMEBODY IN CAMBODIA OR SOMEBODY IN CHINA, AND I WANT THEIR PRODUCT, SO HOW DO I DO COMMERCE WITHOUT MONEY IN THAT SENSE?)

You know. We've only had one quasi-successful monetary system in the history of the world. And that was based on precious metals. But the problem with that, as I said, is that people mistake the symbol of value, for the value.

So whatever you choose, whether it's gold, silver, or

peanuts, that's the standard of value, whatever commodity you choose to establish that benchmark against, is going to be subject to hoarding and manipulation of all kinds, counterfeiting, and blah, blah, blah, blah.

And you are going to set up a situation so whoever has that particular commodity is going to dominate and control and benefit, and everybody else is going to suffer. So it doesn't matter whether it's OPEC, with the oil, or it's the Queen of England, with the gold, or it's Joe Schmo, whose controlling all the legal tender, it just doesn't matter as long as it's based on a commodity, you know, even a basket of commodities. This is the kind of runaround we get.

And we also have the problem of elasticity. I don't know if you ever stop to think about that, but one of the big things that happened in the 19th Century was that with gold and silver, there is only so much, and as a result these, problems accrue when the Need for a medium of exchange, exceeds the supply of that.

And so, coming out of the 19th Century, the big drive for fiat currency is that fiat currencey is elastic. You can print more of it to meet the demand of the market place. So you can have lots of these little symbols running around   serving the needs of the people.

Ok, so I think all of this is crazy. To me it's like I might as well go out at midnight, go out to the tool shed and open up the door and bow down to all the tools.

It's Idolatry. The whole economy is Idolatry. And that's what the Great Abomination is all about. It all started in the ancient Kingdom of Sumer where the Queen of the Sumerians had started doing this. The Sumerians have a lot of grain, and in order to trade, they would have to take baskets of grain from one part of wherever to another part. And they were constantly moving all of this grain around. Right?

She noticed that a basket of grain was trading for the same as a little gold coin in the market place. So she had these little gold coins made, and stamped with a basket of wheat.

And so this came to symbolize a basket of wheat in trade.

It was like a guarantee that there was a basket of wheat in the Sumerian Treasury to back up this little gold coin.

And then we have the Sumerian version of inflation where suddenly it's the same little gold coin, but there are two baskets of wheat stamped on it. And finally, the entire little gold coin is covered with little baskets of wheat, you know.

This is what all this is about. It's idolatry. It's dim-witism. For whatever reason most humans are not able to grasp the symbolism. They don't get it. And so that opens up the possibility of a bunch of shysters getting in there, conmen who disconnect the medium of exchange from the actual fact of what is supposedly being exchanged.

The only way that you can possibly have an honest system of exchange is to include the value of all commodities and all labor, and all natural resourses, roll them up into one big Wad, and let your currency worlwide symbolize that. Otherwise, what happens is the same thing you get with a commodity market.

If you are a producer of the commodity then you have an unfair advantage in the commodity market. And it doesn't matter what commodity it is, because you can sell futures, you can hedge your bets, you can set you prices, you can get together with your buddies and manipulate the market if you have enough market share.

And there are all sorts of things you can do with commodities if you are a producer. But if you're not a producer, you're just a goat. And some countries that have a lot of labor but don't have a lot of natural resources end up as the goats. Right?

UNFORTUNATELY,
THIS INTERVIEW WAS REMOVED FROM THE
INTERNET AT THIS POINT.

**THIS TRANSCRIPT IS NOW CONTINUED HERE:
JUST NOTE WHAT WE WOULD HAVE MISSED BY THIS
TRANSCRIPT BEING CENSORED AND REMOVED.**

They're always the ones who are standing behind the 8-Ball, here. And in order to have a world that is really thriving and healthy, and everybody has what they need, and you don't have poverty, starvation, and disease, and all the miseries that we currently have, is if everybody can bring something to the marketplace and be a producer.

(UM, HM.)

So, you know, if we would set up a system with all of these elements that we treated and were included and were part of the "basket" of commodities, then we could have an honest currency.

Until we do that, we're going to have a situation where, with all this chizeling and manipulation, and hoarding, and, you know, insanity, that has gone on for thousands of years, 8,000 years since Semiramis stamped her little basket of wheat on a gold coin.

And we tried to figure out a better way. And it just strikes me as ridiculous that with as much brain-power and as much technology and everything else that we have now, that we haven't been able to figure our way out of the tool shed, and stop worshiping the tool, and stop worshiping the Creation and start worshiping the Creator.

(AMEN. YOU KNOW, I KEEP ON SAYING AS LONG AS MAN IS GOVERNING MAN, WE'RE NEVER GOING TO HAVE A PERFECT SYSTEM. THAT'S THE WAY IT IS. BECAUSE INHERENTLY, PEOPLE ARE GREEDY AND SELFISH.)

The new "Need and Greed" system is what we have now. What we need is a system that is fair and transparent and honest which allows people to trade whatever there is to trade.

(AND EVERYBODY HAS SOMETHING OF VALUE THAT THEY SHOULD BE ABLE TO TRADE. EVERYBODY DOES. I MEAN YOU CAN FIND SOMETHING WITHIN YOURSELF. BUT IT CHALLENGES PEOPLE TO FIND OUT WHAT THEY HAVE THAT THEY CAN BRING TO THE TABLE. IT'S MY BELIEF THAT EVERYBODY HAS SOMETHING THAT THEY CAN BRING.) (YES. THIS IS A WORLD OF ABUNDANCE AND THERE'S NO WAY THAT A PERSON SHOULD EVER GO TO SLEEP HUNGRY OR WITHOUT A BED, OR WITH-OUT SHELTER, NEVER. IT SHOULD NOT HAPPEN.)

Essentially, it is a blasphemy, because we were given this wonderful world that has an incredible amount of abundance and if anybody is starving or going without it's because of us. It's because we've messed up. It's because we're not doing our job. We're not sharing. We're not figuring things out. Because it's certainly not any lack in our environment.

(I AGREE.) (SO WHAT IS YOUR ADVICE TO PEOPLE? I KNOW, FIRST OF ALL I WOULD SAY THE BIRTH CER-TIFICATE, CLAIM YOUR NAME BACK, AND AFTER THAT WHAT ARE THE NEXT STEPS THAT YOU WOULD SUG-GEST THAT WE TAKE?)

Claim you name back too. I was talking earlier about how they just come by and they arbitrarily assign a name and a number, or whatever description, to your land.

Now, I found out about this in a really strange way. God has prepared me all along the way. He's putting these things in my face.

I was out in my front yard one summer day and this little white car pulled up in the ditch in front of my house and this young lady got out of the car and she had a clipboard.

So I wandered over there and said, "Hi, what are you up to?" She said, "Oh, I'm out assigning street numbers," You know?

(HEY, THAT'S HER JOB. WOW.)

And I talked to her a little bit, and she explained that she's been hired to go out and assign street numbers to all these parcels. And she's just arbitrarily going along . . . "Well, I think I'll call that one 2356 South Park Road, and this one over here, I'll call 2390 South Park Road. Well, does it really matter? I mean, no it doesn't matter. It could be 400, you know, Birchwood Park, if you want."

Hello? She's just arbitrarily out there assigning names to the streets and numbers to the house parcels. Right?

This really gets my wheels running, because I'm thinking . . . let's see, this is the way my land was described on my deed or my, you know, . . . And then I get to digging into it more and I find out, well, there's a plat description, there's a lot-block description, there's a street and number description, you know?

And I paid for all of this! I'm paying at some level of something for all of this.

So, this is just another Scam. This is calling it a Birthday cake, Anniversary cake, and a Merry Christmas cake, and they're expecting someone to pay for all these different cakes, so that all these diferent entities can feed off of you.

But the fact of the matter is that when they took title to our land they took our land out into international jurisdiction and in order to get our land back, to actually own our land, we have to get our own political status straightened out, and identify ourselves as, you know, actual American State Nationals, because US Citizens can't own land in the States. OK?

So, first and foremost, you have to get your own Estate and your own Name back. And then you can get your land back. You can reclaim your land and, Um, go in and do that by doing a metes and bounds survey, a physical survey. You actually attach the description to the physical boundary stones or boundary markers of your land, just like they did back in the day. Right?

And, so you do the metes and bounds and you correct the

deed. You do a deed correction, you give the metes and bounds description, which is the physical land description, and you rename it, and you copyright the name.

So, for example, I paid off anything I owed on my piece of land and I did a deed correction, I did it by the metes and bounds description, you know. You can do the boundary markers. In my case colored boundary markers. And then I arbitrarily named it 4711 Birchwood Road and did my little "c" with the circle around it, my copyright mark, and recorded that.

(AND THAT WAS IT.)

I then copied the tax assessors office. I went over to the tax assessors office. I gave them a copy of my corrected deed, I had them date-stamped in a copy for me so that I could prove that I had actually given notice to them in terms of telling them what I had done. Right?

And then I recorded that.

(AND WHERE DID YOU RECORD THAT?)

With the Land Recording Office.

(AND SO DOES THAT MEAN YOU NO LONGER HAVE PROPERTY TAXES?)

I no longer have property taxes, but I hadn't had property taxes for a number of years prior to that.

Now most of us get a property tax bill every year and we assume that this is for services rendered. Right?

We think about, well, snow plowing, and sanding the roads when they're icy, and cutting the ditches, and, you know, keeping the utility lines clear, and all these different kinds of things, fire services areas, blah, blah, that are provided by the government, the local government. Right?

So this was years ago before I did the metes and bounds, before I corrected the description, before I bearded the tax assessors office in their den, and before I straightened out my own Name and reclaimed my own Estate.

I went to the property tax unit at the local government and I said, "OK, well, you've been providing me with all these services but I don't have a contract with you. So I want to straighten this out. I want to know exactly what I'm paying for and I want to look to see the competition, if I am getting rooked.

(YA, YA, SURE.)

So give me a list of the services that you're providing and how much it's costing me and I'll contract with you for those services that I want, and we'll just do this as a business deal.

(SO THEY WOULDN'T DO IT? LET ME GUESS.)

They didn't reply, and a few days later I sent them another registered letter, and made them this offer, you know, "I realize that you are providing services. I don't want to be unfair or cheat anybody out of anything. I just made the offer to look over the   service that you provide that make sense to me."

Nothing. Zero. You could hear a pin drop. Nothing at all. No reply. So a few days after that I wrote them back and said, "OK, well, I made this offer and I haven't heard from you so I have to assume that you're not interested in contracting to provide services to me, and any services I receive I will accept free gratis.

(AND THEY NEVER CONTACTED YOU AGAIN?) (NO, THAT'S AWESOME. WE'RE GOING TO DO THAT. THIS IS ALL FACINATING STUFF. SORRY WE'RE KEEPING YOU SO LONG. I JUST KNEW I WAS GOING TO BE ASKING A LOT OF QUESTIONS AND GETTING A LOT OF INFORMA-TION.) (I DO HAVE A COUPLE OF OTHER QUESTIONS. AH, THE RIGHT TO TRAVEL, AND TOLLS. WHAT CAN WE DO ABOUT THAT?) (I MEAN, IT DOESN'T SEEM LIKE TOLLS SHOULD BE LEGAL.)

Not if they . . . OK, here's the deal with tolls. They sell off an interest in a road that has been funded by public funds, to private investors, and they [the private investors] put up the toll for the use of that road. Now the question is, did the people who sold that road have the right to do so? And do they have the right to the land under the road? And the answer is about always, No! So then it's another bogus, you know, Make a Buck Scam by the corporations. OK?

So, that's something that will probably be done away with here, but not a real high priority at the moment.

Um. The other thing. The right to travel.

You have the absolute right to travel. The road and Vehicle Code was never designed to do anything to interrupt that, ever. The excuse for the Motor Vehicle Code was Public Safety and the use that certain companies get out of public roads to make private profit.

For example, a taxi cab company, or a long-distance trucking firm, or a courier service. These guys make their living off of your roads---your public resource. Right?

And so that's why they were taxed and that's why they were regulated, licensed. Any time you have a license you are applying to do something that would otherwise be illegal.

(RIGHT) (BECAUSE THEY ARE DRIVERS OF VEHICLES. CORRECT?)

Yes. They are doing this as a profession that's benefitting from a public resource. That's a fact. Right? But when WE drive down to the grocery store that's just me going down to the grocery store. That's me, in my private little auto, going to the grocery store for my private business. Has nothing to do with making any profit off of anybody, or anything. It's just me traveling, and they have no right to say Boo! about that. Nobody has any right to say Boo! about that. So, you're right. You have the absolute right to travel.

Now I have kind of mixed emotions about driver licensing in that I don't approved of licensing driving, you know, for Joe

Average, but on the other hand I DO want to see people acting responsibly . . . that people should know the rules of the road. They just shouldn't be, willy-nilly, out there, you know, ignorantly stumbling around without any training. So I think that if you are going to use the public roads, you should have some training and some capability. You should be able to pass a driving test. OK?

But after that I don't think that you should be licensed. I think you should have an ID and that should be it. Um. Technically we're only required to give our name and our address as an identification.

Now, people come to me all the time because they're being harrassed. They're being pulled over, or they're afraid of being pulled over, and they're afraid of the police, and blah, blah, blah, blah. Well, it's actually their own damned fault because you can stop that. In my case, I put a little Label on my driver's license, and I tell them right there that I'm not a municipal citizen. I'm not using the roads for any profit or gain. OK? I'm retired from all that. OK?

So I have a little label, front and back, on my driver license which says "Retired". That's it. Bye folks.

And everybody at any age can retire from any obligation of citizenship. Citizenship cannot be imposed upon a person against their will. It is a major league war-crime to do so involving piano wire around your neck and a firing squad.

So, you know, they cannot impose citizenship on you. They cannot steal your nationality, you know. You are actually holding the cards. You just don't know that you're holding the cards.

It is the same thing with your car. You are exempt. Your private vehicle, your private car, your auto, is exempt, if you say it is.

If you get Z-plates. . . The regulations of the Vehicle Code that exempts your own [private] car or truck that you're not using for commercial purposes is Regulation "Z". So you go to the Department of Motor Vehicles [some states its Department of Transportation or Department of Public Safety or...] and you say, "I want Z-plates" and they have a little sticker that's a black and white sticker, it says "Z", and it has a Number, and you put it on just like you put on other tags, you know, the renewable tags.

This is a one time only thing. You put it on, BOOM! That identifies it as a private car: [and tells them] that you're claiming your exemption, and then they won't bother you.

(AND ANY STATE OFFICERS?) (HOW MUCH DO THEY COST?)

They cost a little bit more than the renewables. I paid $200 dollars for mine and, normally, I would be paying $160 dollars.

(A YEAR. AND ANYONE CAN APPLY FOR Z-PLATES? OR STICKER?)

Any American.

(SO YOU HAVE GO THROUGH WHAT YOU WANT THEM TO BECOME?)

They'll give you Z-plates, anyway, it doesn't matter.

(AND THEN DO YOU HAVE TO GET YOUR CAR INSPECTED, AND GET TAGS RENEWED AND ALL THAT?) (IF ANYBODY GIVES US A HARD TIME WE'RE GOING TO TELL THEM THAT ANNA TOLD US WE COULD) (CALL JUDGE ANNA BECAUSE SHE SAID WE COULD.)

Just look up the Motor Vehicle Code.

(NO, I'M BAREFOOTED.) (BY THE WAY THIS IS SO MUCH INFORMATION) (I'M TAKING NOTES) (WE'RE GOING TO HAVE YOU BACK ON MULTIPLE TIMES IF YOU WOULD, PLEASE) (SHE'S GOT LIMITED TIME, THOUGH) (I KNOW, EACH ONE OF THESE SUBJECTS IS LIKE AT LEAST 2-HOURS LONG SO WE HAVE JUST TOUCHED THE

SURFACE ON A LOT OF THESE THINGS. WHICH BRINGS ME TO THIS: YOU HAVE A WEBSITE WITH A LOT OF THIS INFORMATION. RIGHT? THAT WE CAN LEARN FROM?)

I am constantly adding to my website, and, you know, as more and more information comes to light we keep adding and amending, and, you know, it's kind of a boiling pot, new insight and new information that comes up. Ah. Right now I'm doing something that people have been asking me to do for a long time, and that is, I'm doing a "step-by-step" for them, going over some of the things that we went over this afternoon.

A detailed explanation. What the birth Certificate is and how it functions, and how to deal with that. And I'll be posting the most updated Certificate of Assumed Name.

If we had more money we could do more. As it stands, we've ferreted out the Sessions laws, not the Statutes, the Sessions laws that govern the common law copyright of assumed names, and we found them in Alaska and Washington State, and a few other States, but because these are federated State Trusts, what's true in one state has to be true in others. OK?

So you can go ahead and do the claiming anyhow, so the thing to post is the Certificate of Assumed Name, the latest and greatest, and people can use that as a template. Just take out my name and, you know, redo it in the same style, and use your own name and your own address, and what-not.

And either record those, or send a record copy to yourself.

There are two ways of recording land jurisdiction documents. One is to record via the land recording office. OK? The other way is the Post Office. Land is International and Soil is National. And what you wind up with is Red ink instead of Blue ink.

Ever notice that a Postage Stamp and a Cancellation Stamp is always red? That's a Land jurisdiction. A stamp that you see coming out of their Courts, those are always blue: sea jurisdiction. OK?

So, anyway, when you get your Certificate of Assumed Name done, you can take it to the local Land Recording Office. Some of them object and won't record it unless it has the Session Law from that particular state, and you can either pay a Para-legal to go dig up that Session Law regarding guaranteeing your copyright right for an assumed name or you can send yourself a record copy.

I prefer to get it straight, look up the law and cite it, and get it recorded in the public Land Recording Office, this is what I did, but you can also send yourself a record copy.

And this applies to anything that you want to get a record of. You send yourself a registered letter and when it comes back you just put it in the file along with your file copy of whatever is in that letter. And if any question comes up you certify a copy of the file copy you have, that this is a true complete and correct copy of the document, blah, blah.

Sign and Date it: by Anna Maria Riezinger [Your Trade Name]. Then you can walk in and you have this little envelope and you wave it at the judge. Here, I have a record copy, a sealed record copy.

You have absolute proof that you sent this and you have the registration number from the registered mailing which is the record number, and you have the red stamp.

So, when it comes to any altercation with the court, that's as good as having it recorded at the Land Jurisdiction Office. So if you can't get it recorded at the land recorder's office, because they're being buttheads, you can always do a registered mailing to yourself.

(BEAUTIFUL.) (THERE IS A WAY.) (OH, YA.) (WOW.) (IN-CREDIBLE INFORMATION.) (WELL, YOU KNOW, WE'VE KEPT YOU SO LONG. I'M GONNA. JUST LET ME END BY SAYING THIS BECAUSE YOU HAVE ALLUDED A FEW TIMES TO A LOT OF CHANGES COMING UP. AND WHAT CHANGES ARE COMING UP? AND I KNOW WE COULD GO ON FOR ANOTHER HOUR, BUT JUST HIGH LEVEL CHANGES THAT ARE COME UP. WHO ARE INITIATING THE

CHANGES? HOW DEFINITE ARE THESE CHANGES?) (AND IS THERE ANTHING WE CAN DO TO HELP?) (OH, YA.)

The biggest change is that my husband kicked them in the pants and let them know that the presumed interregnum of our government has ended, and never really was. So they've just been saying and telling the rest of the world that our government is an interregnum. It's taking a break. It's on pause, for 150 years.

So, as it turns out, his ancestors are the ones that donated, I won't say "donated", they took the fledgling Republic and they, Ah, basically acted as Heads of State. And all of the Great Seal, and all of that, is under their Coat of Arms array . . . under their kingship. And so he just, hm. He had enough of it and sent out a notice that the interregnum is ended, if it ever existed, and issued a Proclamation to go with it that detailed a lot of this. And so that is a big change.

That's a huge change. That's Noticing the world that the body politic is still here. And No. We haven't abandoned our land or our property or anything else, and all you grubby bankers and all you charlatan lawyers can just get back into your little box and stay there because we're not putting up with it any more.

(SO THE NOTICE HAS BEEN PUT OUT THERE.) (HAS THERE BEEN RECOGNITION?)

Of course.

So that's a big change. Another big change. We expressly stated that our Currency is the American Silver Dollar. Hello!

And maybe that should not be big news, but it is, because, you know, for a long time everybody was assuming it was the Federal Reserve Note.

We located the Record when the US Navy Municipal Corporation infringed on our copyright and created a corporation called UNITED STATES OF AMERICA, in all caps, and if you'll notice, that is what they have on their Federal Reserve

Note. And that is their excuse for trying to charge us for all of their debt. So we seized upon that trademark and we put it in trust, we likened it. That's a big change.

(AND THAT WAS RECORDED AND ALL LEGAL AND THAT'S BEEN PUT INTO PLACE OK?) (DAMN! RECORDED. BOOM.)

And, ah, let's see?

(SO WHEN IS THIS GOING TO AFFECT THE COMMON PERSON? MY NEIGHBOR?)

Maybe as soon as you all get your paperwork in order, and learn how to use it. You're going to be driving these judges absolutely crazy. They're going to run off their bench. All these bill collectors, the IRS, they're going to get back into their little box. They're gonna get back into their little box.

(SO, I'VE SEEN THE IRS GO BACK.) (SO, THIS IS INDI-VIDUAL EMPOWERMENT YOU'RE TALKING ABOUT. ONE PERSON AT A TIME TAKING BACK THEIR OWNERSHIP. I GOT IT. BECAUSE EVERYBODY SHOULD BE RESPON-SIBLE FOR THEIR OWN ACTIONS.)

That's self-governing! Presto! You got it!

(WELL, I GOT IT. DID YOU SEE THE LIGHTBULB THAT WENT OFF OVER MY HEAD? ALL OF A SUDDEN IT'S SO BRIGHT IN HERE!)

Right! So you've got to get busy and get it all done.

(WELL, WE'RE GETTING BUSY TOMORROW.) (I LIKE IT.) (SO, JUDGE ANNA, THANK YOU SO MUCH FOR ALL THE INFORMATION YOU GAVE US. AND THANK YOU FOR ALL YOUR TIME. AND WE KNOW THAT YOU HAVE

LIMITED TIME, SO WE APPRECIATE YOUR COMING IN AND WE DEFINITELY WANT YOU TO COME BACK ON, AT SOME POINT.) (YOU'RE A BREATH OF FRESH AIR, AND SO MUCH KNOWLEDGE, AND OUR AUDIENCE IS GOING TO LOVE YOU, AND WE ALL THANK YOU SO MUCH!)

Take care. I hope I helped and didn't confuse people too much.

(IT SEEMED LIKE YOU WERE VERY CLEAR ABOUT EVERYTHING. I UNDERSTOOD EVERTHING CLEARLY, AND I TOOK A LOT OF NOTES, AND I'LL BE POSTING THEM INTO THE DESCRIPTION, AND I'LL ALSO DIRECT THEM TO YOUR WEBSITE WHICH WILL BE A BIG HELP.)

Well, I'd like to see if you can drum up some extra donations for us because right now, we're really hard hit, and I know that everybody is looking at taxes and everything else. I've got several dollars in my account to take care of 20 people.

(NOW TELL PEOPLE HOW TO DONATE.)

I have a PayPal account at *avannavon@gmail.com* and I have a snail mail address: and checks should be made out to **Anna Maria Riezinger, c/o P.O.Box 520994, Big Lake, Alaska 99652**.

I think it's important for people to know that all of this has been done out of pocket by just average Americans, like them, and that's a huge expense over the years, not to mention all of the hours that have gone into this that have never been paid.
And I've got a Group, the LIVING LAW FIRM, people who have been judges [and lawyers] who have torn up their BAR Cards and said enough of this, and have taken up the fight.
And there's also researchers, historical researches who have been financial auditors, CPAs, wonderful people that have come forward and helped unravel all of this and make this

possible. But they've all been unpaid.

(IS THIS PART OF THE 20 PEOPLE THAT YOUR TALK-ING ABOUT?)

Well, ya. I've got 20 people who need help. I've got probably 150 who are, like me, wanting to do it without taking out of the kitty. I've got some really bright young men who have families who are donating vast amounts of time with this and we need their help but we can't pay them a salary, so what we do is we try to pay bills that come up.

We just had a dental emergency for one of the wives, and we had a child that broke her arm, and we have money to get the arm set, and things like this come up.

But if you don't have a salaried job, if you're working to free America, and this is what we do, we try to help them with things like that, so if they need a little extra for their food budget, we give them that much, because we can't afford to hire them. Right? But now we use the donations for that kind of expenses that we can help them with.

(WE HAVE A GREAT SUBSCRIBERSHIP SO WE'LL DO WHATEVER WE CAN TO GET THE MESSAGE OUT, AND TO HELP YOU GUYS. AND ONCE AGAIN, I WANT TO THANK YOU FOR YOUR TIME. I REALLY APPRECIATE IT. AND THANK YOU FOR ALL THE INFORMATION. GOD BLESS YOU, AND HAVE A GREAT HOLIDAY SEASON.)

(AND I WAS TRYING TO TAKE NOTES, BUT IF YOU WOULDN'T MIND, WOULD YOU SEND ME AN E-MAIL WITH THAT STUFF WRITTEN OUT SO I CAN BE SURE I GET EVERTHING CORRECT. AND I'LL PUT IT IN THE DESCRIP-TION SO THAT EVERYBODY CAN BE SURE TO GET THAT AND SEND DONATIONS TO YOU.)

Okay. Thank You.

(THANK YOU SO MUCH. HAVE A GREAT NIGHT.)

Alright . . .

America: Some Assembly Required
Authored by Anna Maria Riezinger,
Designed by David E Robinson

5.5" x 8.5" (13.97 x 21.59 cm)
Black & White on White paper
60 pages
ISBN-13: 978-1984292360
ISBN-10: 1984292366
BISAC: Political Science / Corruption
& Misconduct

An explosive blockbuster Indictment
of the evil corruptions of America
affecting the world.

https://www.amazon.com/America-Assembly-Anna-Maria-
Riezinger/dp/1984292366/
ref=sr_1_3?s=books&ie=UTF8&qid=1519250440&sr=1-
3&keywords=america+some+assembly+required

Forming Jural Assemblies: Building Blocks of the Republic
Authored by David E. Robinson

5.5" x 8.5" (13.97 x 21.59 cm)
Black & White on White paper
108 pages
ISBN-13: 978-1460922521
(CreateSpace-Assigned)
ISBN-10: 1460922522
BISAC: Political Science / Political Freedom & Security / Law Enforcement

We The People are the First Level of Government in a Republic.

As one of We The People you can see how you, in a Jural Assembly, have Power and Authority "over" your elected free state officials of "state government" through your State/Settlement Constitution.

Your State/Settlement Constitution is the road map of authority for your elected free state "Officials" which includes the "process" by which you have the power and the authority to "hire and fire" these "servants."

In your State/Settlement Constitution you need to make provision for you, the We The People, to have the power

https://www.amazon.com/Forming-Jural-Assemblies-Building-Republic/dp/1460922522/ref=asap_bc?ie=UTF8

Disclosure 101: What You Need To Know
Authored by David E. Robinson,
Original author Anna von Reitz

5" x 8" (12.7 x 20.32 cm)
Black & White on White paper
270 pages
ISBN-13: 978-1500352011
(CreateSpace-Assigned)
ISBN-10: 1500352012
BISAC: Political Science / Government / General

The American Republic:
The United States of America (major)
= the united States of America = uSA =
50 States joined in perpetual Union by
the Articles of Confederation via the
Northwest Ordinance and the Equal
Footing Doctrine = organic geographi-
cally described states = living inhabit-
ants = American Nationals = john-
quincy:doe or John Quincy of the
Family Doe = names of living people =
heirs; beneficiaries; entitlement hold-
ers; priority creditors = private sector =
Law of the Land = The Constitution
for the united States of America = The
United States of America in Congress
Assembled = congress of the United
States of America = unincorporated
Trust Management Company doing
business as The United States = Body

https://www.amazon.com/Disclosure-101-What-Need-Know/dp/
1500352012/ref=asap_bc?ie=UTF8

You Know Something Is Wrong When: An American Affidavit of Probable Cause
Authored by Anna Maria Riezinger, and James Clinton Belcher
Illustrated by Paul Alan Snover

8.5" x 11" (21.59 x 27.94 cm)
Full Color Bleed on White paper
276 pages
ISBN-13: 978-1514757383
ISBN-10: 1514757389
BISAC: Political Science / Government / National

An Affidavit of Probable Cause for Idictments

https://www.amazon.com/You-Know-Something-Wrong-When/dp/1491279184/ref=asap_bc?ie=UTF8

From Debt To Prosperity: 'Social Credit' Defined

Authored by David E. Robinson

5.5" x 8.5" (13.97 x 21.59 cm)
Black & White on White paper
222 pages
ISBN-13: 978-1453835494
(CreateSpace-Assigned)
ISBN-10: 1453835490
BISAC: Education / Finance

There is no reason for us to put up with recession, depression and unemployment. The government simply has to put more money into circulation.

It can all be paid for if the government increased the money supply by issuing national, debt-free money, as Lincoln did at the start of the Civil War.

We suffer from a failure of consumer demand because of a lack of buying power - because of our failure to use our God-given national credit to prime the pump.

Our country was pulled out of the Depression by priming the pump with liquidity and funding new projects that put new money into the people's pocket.

https://www.amazon.com/Debt-Prosperity-Social-Credit-Defined/dp/1453835490/ref=asap_bc?ie=UTF8

**Reclaim Your Sovereignty: Take
Back Your Christian Name**
Authored by David E. Robinson

5.5" x 8.5" (13.97 x 21.59 cm)
Black & White on White paper
128 pages
ISBN-13: 978-1449967499
(CreateSpace-Assigned)
ISBN-10: 1449967493
BISAC: Political Science / Public
Policy / Social Policy

Disillusionment is the dissolution of
an illusion and a return to wonder, to
innocence, and to truth.

What is "the red pill"? The red pill is a
term used in the movie The Matrix, to
refer to "The undistorted truth."

What distorts truth? False belief.

The phase "I don't believe it" implies
that something is evident but that one
does not or will not accept it because
the evidence does not fit an existing
belief (i.e. and existing denial).

"I don't believe it" is often the first
thing someone says when he eventu-
ally accepts that which becomes
obvious to him in due time.

https://www.amazon.com/Reclaim-Your-Sovereignty-Take-Chris-
tian/dp/1449967493/ref=asap_bc?ie=UTF8

**JUDGE ANNA VON REITZ - TAKING BACK AMERICA -
Exclusive Full Interview W/ Victurus Libertas**

It's BACK !!! Taking Back America - !!! JUDGE ANNA VON REITZ
- Subscribe & support VL https://www.patreon.com/victuruslibertas
We will burn this to DVD by request without the Advertisement in
the beginning. Email me at: victuruslibertas@gmail.com. All Patreons
$10 & Up will get one by request free of charge.
Judge Anna's website www.annavonreitz.com
Here's her PayPal: avannavon@gmail.com
Anna Maria Riezinger c/o Box 520994 Big Lake, Alaska 99652

https://www.youtube.com/watch?v=R3QyMj5_FjI&t=4759s

www.ingramcontent.com/pod-product-compliance
Lightning Source LLC
Chambersburg PA
CBHW051922250726
48659CB00002B/796